LET'S GO!
To the Airport

Written by Lisa Harkrader
Illustrated by Jane Miles-Smith
Cover illustrated by Louise Gardner

Louis Weber, C.E.O., Publications International, Ltd.
7373 North Cicero Avenue, Lincolnwood, Illinois 60712

Ground Floor, 59 Gloucester Place, London W1U 8JJ

Customer Service: 1-800-595-8484 or customer_service@pilbooks.com

www.pilbooks.com

Permission is never granted for commercial purposes.

p i kids is a registered trademark of Publications International, Ltd.

ISBN-13: 978-1-4127-9175-5
ISBN-10: 1-4127-9175-8

8 7 6 5 4 3 2 1

publications international, ltd.

My name is Captain Miles. I'm an airplane pilot.

My job is to fly airplanes from one airport to another. I fly a large passenger jet to cities all over the world.

An airport is a busy place. It is open every single day of the year. Airplanes take off and land at the airport all day and all night.

I wear a uniform and cap so people know I am a pilot.

The four gold stripes on my cuffs and on the shoulders of my coat show that I am a captain.

The captain is the senior member of an airplane crew.

I worked as a copilot, or first officer, for many years before I was qualified and ready to become a captain.

Passengers arrive at the airport one to two hours before their flights leave. They usually go to the ticket counter first. Every passenger needs a ticket to ride on an airplane. Some passengers buy tickets before they come to the airport. Some buy tickets at the ticket counter. They can also check in their suitcases at the ticket counter.

Checked-in suitcases travel on a conveyor belt to the baggage handling area. Baggage handlers inspect the suitcases, sort them, and load them into the cargo area of the airplane.

Food-service workers may load meals and drinks onto the airplane. The cleaning crew makes sure everything is tidy. They also load magazines and pillows.

My copilot and I arrive at the airport about an hour before our flight. We go to the pilot's lounge, where we map the route we will fly. Then we find out what the weather will be like.

I write a detailed flight plan and give it to air traffic control. Air traffic control tracks all flights and keeps airplanes from having accidents.

Passengers board airplanes through gates. They walk through metal detectors to get to their gates. They send their briefcases, purses, and small items through an X-ray machine. The X-ray machine shows what is inside each item. Security officers make sure the items do not hold anything that is not allowed onboard an airplane.

The airplane crew boards the plane before passengers begin boarding. Flight attendants help passengers find their seats. They tell the passengers how to stay safe on the airplane.

My copilot and I sit in the front of the plane, in an area called the cockpit. The cockpit has all the controls we need to fly the plane.

In the cockpit, we have a radio so we can talk to the control tower. When it is safe to take off, we pull away from the gate and taxi onto the runway. It's our turn to take off!